360 Woman

Elizabeth Niko

Please direct all copyright inquiries to:
B.O.Y. Enterprises, Inc.
c/o Author Copyrights
P.O. Box 262
Lowell, NC 28098

Paperback ISBN: 978-1-955605-48-9

Cover and Interior Design: B.O.Y. Enterprises, Inc.

Printed in the United States.

Dedication

This has been the hardest thing I've ever had to do… opening my life and my thoughts beliefs to the world.

360 Woman was inspired by Proverbs 31:10-31

TABLE OF CONTENTS

A MESSAGE TO THE READER ------------------------- 7

CHAPTER ONE --- 8

CHAPTER TWO -- 19

CHAPTER THREE--- 26

CHAPTER FOUR --- 31

FINALE -- 35

360 TRAINING EXERCISE TRAINING --------------- 38

A Message to the Reader

Dear Reader,

I pray this book inspires and encourages you, while producing transformation and a positive powerful change for you in a very grandiose way. I have to admit I'd never thought I'd experience the challenges I have in writing this book. The heartbreaks, heartaches, setbacks, disappointments, life challenging test, discovered insecurities, and fear of failure which were uncovered writing this book have been unreal but yet real. This experience allows you to know what kind of get up and fight you have inside of you. It pushes you to change your mindset, to be positive, to think; speak; see; and envision life until you make manifest by pressing your way out of an uncomfortable situation. Through the writing of this book, I've learned to focus forward on only what's important, become a student of myself, and walk in my 360 Power and gifts God has given me.

Now that I have experienced this transformational journey, I desire to share it with all of you. I'm challenging you to raise your hands up high and ask the Lord, which one of these gifts right now are you going to use inside of me to get me out of this uncomfortable situation into a comfortable one. Lord make Manifest Now ….

Your Sister in Christ,

Elizabeth Niko

Chapter One

Dear God, allow me to be transparent open and honest while writing this book. Allow this information to help me and all who read it become better and no longer allow ourselves to be 180 chics. But finally become the full circle well rounded 360 woman who You created us to be. Father, God be with me, be my strength, and my guide in the revealing of my truth Thank you Lord. Amen

Okay look peeps, I am not perfect at all. I'm still trying to figure this life out just like you. At 46 years of age, I'm broken but I'm determined to be fixed. I just heard the voice of the Lord say write this book and I have absolutely no idea what I'm doing! (lol. I'm laughing but I'm serious.) I'm being obedient and writing this short book of what He has revealed to me. This awesome information is for our betterment, so if you're ready to take this leap of faith and go on this obedience journey with me… here we go.

I'm so inspired by Proverbs 31:10-31, the sayings of King Lemuel's Mother instilled in him. This woman was Gangster to me! She broke it down to her son in an "Inspired Utterance."

> **Utterance:**
> A spoken word, statement, or vocal sound.
> The action of saying something aloud.
> The uninterrupted chain of spoken or written language.

Have you ever stopped to consider your own vocal sound? Is it positive? Is it negative? Is it doubt, criticism, fussing, accusing, keeping it real (Lol that kills me), gossip, or is it love? Is it encouraging yourself and others?

Your thoughts and your words are connected. Both are very powerful so whatever we think and speak we bring to life or death. This includes what we think and speak about our lives, relationships, children, family, students, and our business.

Okay let's start here Proverbs 10:1-2

A wife a woman of noble character, who can find her?

Definition: Having or showing fine personal qualities, high moral standards, principals, ideals.

Huh? Imagine an emoji confused face here. That's how I looked when I read it. I bet your expression is similar. I really had to stop and question myself with this, I looked up and asked the Lord, "Okay JAH, be straight with me. Am I noble or at least something like a noble woman? Heck do I even actually know any noble chics at all ???"

9

Answer: Nope, Nah. Okay, okay God. Well, let's fix that.

"I mean I'm no moralist but let's get to the fixing of me then the fixing of my circle. Lord please, I don't want to be boring and fake through this okay Yahweh." Then I blew him kisses. Muah Muah

Late 2018 I started profiling myself getting to know and investigating who Elizabeth Niko is. I needed to know what I'm attracted to and what is attracted to me. I also needed to know what I allow, where my weakness lies, what makes me move, as well as what my turn ons and turn offs are. And the scariest part to deal with was where my insecurities lie, my secrets.

If I'm honest with you and myself, I'm afraid to finish what I start because I'm afraid of failure.

I feel forgotten, unloved, and rejected. I feel angry a lot. I just want to assassinate anyone who defames my character or tries to hurt me. Yeah, I know it's not right, but it's real.

But here's the irony I'm mad confident! I actually love myself. I figured out how to love me through it all and I adore myself. I love people. I enjoy helping and giving to others. I want to give the lost, the forgotten, the ignored, the rejected, and the abused everything I didn't get.

I told myself the past pain/hurts made me stronger.

I turned that "Assassin Spirit" that wants to bust ninja moves on folks into passion/purpose/creativity. Now I can tell the lost… they're found, the rejected… they're accepted, the forgotten… hey I remember you. I turned my pain into profitable entrepreneurship. I'm a serial entrepreneur and business strategist.

Creating businesses out of nothing became my obsession… my addiction… my distraction. But no matter how distracted, I couldn't shake the fact that God says I'm not noble and it made sense why the money from business came easy, but also developed wings fast. The money was easy come, easy go. Child that was a hard pill to swallow! Every year it felt like I was going from the top of the mountain back to the bottom. Even now, as I write this book, I feel like I am still going through the same up and down cycle.

This unstable cycle was exhausting, mentally, physically, emotionally. Easy go was heart shattering. Building a great business just to continue this cycle of losing it shook my spirit. But I also knew I could change this. I was determined to be noble, to be a wise woman. I began to dig deep into the word of God. I wanted to know what makes this virtuous woman so great. I was so drawn to the Proverbs 31 woman that I began to study what was written and uttered about her. I was desperate to change my character and I believed studying her would show me how.

As I studied, literally every verse was speaking to me, so I read it every day over and over. I studied it and the revelation, God's intel, dropped into my spirit as a heavenly Spoken Word… "Elizabeth Niko if you're ready to stop being a 180 chic and become a full circle 360 woman, follow these principles. There are instructions, guidelines, and valuable information that's imperative to you walking out your success, your passion, what you were created for, and how to get chosen… meaning get your mate."

WOW! Alright Lord well let's drive this car and turn the wheel 360! Let's make doughnuts! So, I hit the gas, then I visualized myself in my spiritual and physical Maserati SUV, with some fly shades on from my line of shades, leather gloves even though my nails were done to perfection, music booming, and I said loudly putting prophetic action to my faith, "Now let's get my noble on!" I know its corny, but its real.

Enter the "so what had happened was" part. This is when things got real!

So once upon a time I had this underground, off the radar Boutique called *Bag And Boujee*. I was going hard selling high end high-quality replica bags and accessories to my clientele. It was Tony The Tiger Greatttttt, to the tune of about $3.5K a day. The whole time I was feeding my adrenaline selling merchandise, I heard the Lord saying, "Niko, you're working on being noble. The knock off biz has to cease now."

Huh? Now Lord? You want me to stop now when business is booming?

You see… I felt as if I was protected from anything bad happening to my business because (here's the funny part) I'm a tither, a cheerful giver. I attend Lakewood church. Bill Winston is my YouTube Pastor. I believed I was so covered in the Blood of Jesus that I was impenetrable and untouchable. Lol

Nope! God spoke to me again, "Elizabeth Niko, stop selling the knock off and go legit!"

So, I thought I could out smart God, bribe Him or distract Him by creating a fashion line called the Foster Brand. That way I had legit and knock offs. I thought this was an easy solution. The Foster Brand went well too, but not as well as *Bag And Boujee*. I had gotten greedy, so greedy I wouldn't take heed or be obedient to God's command. I'd grown so full of myself, I figured I could make God a very noble proposition. Lol

"Okay Lord. So, I'm just going to keep *Bag and Boujee* open one more month make another $15k or so. Then I will be at $100k. Then I will stop. Okay God?" Then I blew Him a kiss. Muah

That was on a Friday. I had just received a big shipment too. Lawd Jesus I could feel the money! I felt like the Queen of The South Filp'n Bricks. Clients were coming in and out buying me out. I'm like yes! I'm almost at my goal! Then on

Saturday evening my middle daughter, Asiannah, came into my room and said to me, "Mom, God told me to tell you shut *Bag And Boujee* down now or something bad is going to happen." I could have died at that moment because I thought the only voice Asia, listened to was Nicki Minaj. I was so nervous but yet I was still negotiating my noble character that I asked God for.

"Okay God," I said. "I'll stop by Monday." My daughter was so disappointed in me continuing to sell knock offs. Late Sunday afternoon Asia said to me, "Mom can you please just not sell anything today?" I ignored her and guess who came knocking at my door… The police aka "the popo" accompanied by Louis Vuitton authenticators with a nice warrant to search the premises and arrest me.

I closed my eyes and click my heels together 3 times. It wasn't a dream and nope they still didn't go away. Long story short, the same daughter that gave me the warning talked the police out of arresting me or pressing charges on me. So, I kept my freedom, but that freedom came with a price. They left with all my hard earned $95k and whatever merchandise I had left! SMH

Man… the cost of disobedience is hard! At that moment, I was sick and tired of my rebellious, greedy, disobedient 180 ass! I was done being a failure by fault of my own. Because of my disobedience, my ignorance, this cycle of self-induced failure was shattering. The disappointment in my kids' eyes was even worse. I lost our money, our home, and our car.

We had to move in with a fake friend who was literally the devil's bride.

Talking about cracking the whip, I was literally scared straight. I had to repent and "**Now faith**" my way out of this horrible situation. I had to change my mind set to retain my mind and not go crazy and that's just what I did. I picked up my bible got right into the word of God. I went right back into Proverbs because I needed wisdom, comprehension, and strategy of what God was instructing me to be. I needed God to teach me how to live because without comprehension and strategy there is no manifestation.

So now I can raise my hand high if you ask who can find a noble woman! I am Her! I am noble with legitimate business affairs only. And in the transition, I discovered me, my passions, my gifts, and talents. I discovered things that I absolutely love to do and how to bottle it, bag it, tag it and sell it baby.

It started with consistent mental thoughts brain exercise, consistently thinking positive thoughts and speaking them out of my mouth and creating vision boards. I also listened to Dr. Yalonda C. Wilson, Dr. Bill Winston, John Gray, Dr. Caroline Leaf, Joel Osteen, Kenneth Copland, Cindy Trimm, Pastor Toure & Sarah Jakes Roberts, TD Jakes, Creflo Dollar , Jessie Duplantis, Jerry Servell, Dr. Marie Baptiste, and Veronica Abisay. I studied the word and the messages they ministered. I heard, I declared, and spoke it.

I made vision boards and turned them into **NOW FAITH** boards until it was no longer a struggle to be that noble woman. I made my decision to be a ***360 woman*** and not to be a 180 chic ever again. I finally know who I am and what I'm not.

I could still hear very faintly what use to be. It's the loud voice of my dad in my mind saying, "Niko everybody has a price." My father believed that anybody would sell their soul for the right amount of money no matter the cost. But I was finally free from believing that about myself. I finally knew my worth as a woman and a beautiful brilliant black woman! My price is worth more than rubies. Proverbs 31:10 NIV

I am a 360 Woman

I am priceless.
I am secure and confident.
I lack absolutely nothing in value.
I am obedient, loyal, and trustworthy.
I am drama free, no popo knocking at my door any longer.
I am for God and my fellow man, not against them.

Notes

What comes up for you after reading this chapter? Take a moment to reflect on what you read and record your thoughts.

_____

_____

_____

_____

_____

_____

_____

_____

_____

_____

_____

_____

_____

_____

_____

_____

_____

_____

_____

_____

_____

_____

Chapter Two

The Business Strategist, Solutionist

Strategy

"She selects wool and flax and works eagerly with her hands. She is like merchant ships, bringing her food from afar." **-Proverbs 31:13-14 NIV**

I want to talk about this virtuous noble woman, this Boss. She's a buyer. She has a keen eye for what the people want. She has eager hands. She's anxious and can't wait to get the product out to the people because she knows it's good and she really wants to get it into your hands. She has no time for excuses. She seizes her moment because she knows the value of time. She's ready to put it together, plan the event, get it pop'n. She is Martha Stewart on Jesus!

This woman is like merchant ships, buying selling, trading, a watercraft that transports cargo all over the world, online, in stores, and outside markets. Her products, merchandise, investments, and land, are all over the world. She is a serial entrepreneur, and master negotiator. She knows how to get the best for less, nothing but the best for her family, friends, and clients because she knows she is royalty.

Reading those scriptures, I found that I really needed to know what my passion was, what my gifts were, and what I really loved to do. I have a passion for the entertainment industry, creating shows, and recognizing stars a needle in a haystack. I also love cooking, fashion, motivating the masses, being creative, inventing, building, and giving. I can literally create a business out of anything and make an instant profit right away. I discovered my gifts and talents by researching myself.

Research yourself and your passions. Don't be a copycat! Get your own identity, stand out, plant your seed in the soil that was created for your seed to grow. Start with your own sprout, then you will flourish.

Okay 360 Women, here are your instructions. I'm going to repeat Proverbs 31:13. She selects wool and flax and works with eager hands. Pay close attention to every sentence in this scripture. Every word is your remedy for your success is in it.

360 Woman selects wool and flax. What is wool and flax?

It's one seed that does many different things. It blooms into the blue flower called (Herbaceous flax annual plants). This is where her linen, wool, flax comes from, this amazing multi-purpose seed planted in the ground (soil). I felt compelled to research this plant a little further and I'm going to share a little bit more with you but just a little. I'm not going to do all the work for you 360 reader. You're going to have to do the research yourself. I'm just leading you to the water, it's up to you to drink. ☺

This passage that says she selects wool and flax intrigues me so much. These beautiful seeds turned into materials come from this marvelous miraculous multi-purpose Herbaceous plant, an annual flower that is cultivated for its seed. The plant is made into textile fiber, known in Western countries as linen, bed sheets, under clothes, table linen. The Herbaceous plant even produces Flax seed, oils, medicine, carrots, potatoes, mint, and even bananas!

Wow! Seriously, this 360 woman has discovered 360 seeds. She is a business genius! Who would have thought of or discovered one plant with so many unique purposes? There is not a doubt in my mind that this virtuous, noble, 360 woman was more than a billionaire. She was a seed, a vessel of God that consistently received downloads from Heaven, chatted with God, and figured out that she was one seed who has several different purposes, many gifts, many talents, many abilities to do many remarkable things. She knew that with God all things are possible. (Luke 1:37 NIV)

360 reader, do you see where I'm going with this revelation? We are just like this plant, one seed with many different purposes. We are all multitalented creators.

Now once she selects her wool and flax, the bible says she works with eager hands. That word eager stands out and tells me this 360 woman is anxious, impatient, longing, yearning, aching, thirsty, hopeful, hungry, greedy, wishing, wanting to do or have something very much. She was very eager to get the word from God that would produce the seed in her hands to get out to the people. This 360 virtuous career woman was a buyer. She had an eye for what the people wanted and what they needed.

"She is like merchant ships bringing her food from afar."
-Proverbs 31:14 NIV

I read this passage over and over and got so many revelations I had to define it and break it down. A merchant ship we know is a trading vessel, a watercraft that transports cargo. Now here's the Rhema... this awesome, amazing, intriguing woman is a serial entrepreneur with many streams of income! She has heavenly money, (now faith is her currency) and natural money and lots of both because it takes great faith confidence in God to stand in the office she is in. She's only putting best in her body, eating right, serving the best, healthiest, succulent, tastiest foods to her family, friends, ministry, servants, and clients. She is being creative with what she serves. Her cookbook is so good and creative making you yearn for the best. The Bible's cookbook is straight from Heaven's kitchen! Let's call it recipes from Jesus or by Jesus. Lol

The Download

Proverbs 31:15 She gets up while it is still night; 4:30 AM,

That is a very imperative time. This is the time she is praying, seeking God, receiving instructions, worshiping the Lord, downloading all that He has for her marriage, her family, her household, her staff, ministry, businesses, and inventions. She downloads intel from Heaven for the day and the days to come. She gets the agenda for her life, her purpose, and her destiny. She is having intimate time with God asking Him, "Lord what is my assignment? What will you have your servant do? How can I serve you?"

She digs deep into the word of God, dissecting every word renewing her mind daily. Because this 360 woman knows she cannot have success without the daily downloads and the daily renewing of her mind. She knows she has to do this because this is the secret the very root of her success.

360 women, our greatest enemy is ignorance. What you don't know will hurt you. Not making time for God when we first wake up is dangerous for us. It allows the enemy to sneak in make us unbalanced and cause us to trust in the wrong things. I can't express enough how important this part is for our lives.

Because she rises early and downloads from Heaven, she knows just what to plan and prepare for her family and for her servants. So, she begins her day with a daily plan. I absolutely love this woman. She is truly my mentor! Now this next part always knocks my socks off.

> *"She considers a field and buys it; out of her own earnings she plants a vineyard."* **-Proverbs 31:16 NIV**

Do you realize how huge this revelation is? This amazing woman has vision. She's able to just look at a field and visualize what it is going to be! She buys it with her own money. This lets me know she's a Millionaire, maybe even a billionaire with CEO authority to buy at will what she wants. Notice the scripture didn't say she had to ask her husband first. She already downloaded and asked God. He gave her the okay plan at 4:30AM. She has spiritual insight, a heads up that it's all good for her seeds to be planted there and create a vineyard for her awesome wine line called the first miracle from water to wine.

She's not worried about being fussed at by her husband or the accountant. She's not even worried about the price. Why? Because she walks by faith and with no fear or being uneasy. She buys the next business, creating generational wealth for her family, ministry, and charities. She's motivation to future women of the world that will follow in her footsteps.

Notes

What comes up for you after reading this chapter? Take a moment to reflect on what you read and record your thoughts.

_____

_____

_____

_____

_____

_____

_____

_____

_____

_____

_____

_____

_____

_____

_____

_____

_____

_____

_____

_____

_____

_____

Chapter Three

Proverbs 31:17 she sets about her work vigorously, her arms are strong for her task.

This verse right here really spoke loudly to me. I literally researched every word. I was so shocked that the bible expresses she is physically fit. She works out! She pushes herself in a daily vigorous workout so that she can be strengthened for all her tasks physically, mentally, and spiritually. There is no way possible her arms are strong for the task if she's not working out.

Lamp

Proverbs 31:18, *she is so pleased with her business dealings she knows she did well, and her lamp does not go out at night.*

What does that mean? It means because of her daily download, she has the source of spiritual intellectual light inside of her the lamp of learning which allows her to have God like power (see Psalms 82:6). Her body continues to give of light. Everywhere she goes, she is a torch, the moon, a bright star. She is the same all the time, not just for the people, but for her family for the God she loves. She doesn't change.

> **Note:** When you stay in the spirit realm you make no mental time for insecurities. You are permanently tatted with confidence, strength, honor, dignity.

Proverbs 31:19 *in her hands she holds the distaff, and grasped the spindle with her fingers* (see gathering supplies Proverbs 31:13)

Now let's get down to business. It's time to get to work. Remember in verse 13, she's selecting wool and flax and is excited to work with her new materials? She's ready to create and design. Okay, so this is how I see it in present day… she has her sewing machines and workers ready to work with the linen material so she can create her lifestyle brand, which is clothing, under garments, tablecloths, mouth wash, sashes, and so much more! She is constantly creating for her business. The mission is creation, and she is excelling at it!

Proverbs 31:20 *she opens her arms to the poor and extends her hands to the needy.*

She has the heart of God when it comes to giving to the poor and the needy. She is always giving and teaching them how to have for a lifetime instead of a day. She's not afraid, nor is she too proud to go down to the lowest end of town and minister to the people and supply them with what they need. She is always giving without hesitation. This 360 woman will go the extra mile. She's a residual giver.

Proverbs 31:21 *When it snows, she has no fear for her household; for all of them are clothed in scarlet.*

Let's call this conversation Scarlett. I'm such a red fan but I know why now more than ever. As I read this particular verse, I wondered why she wasn't worried about the snow, it's cold. And why did it matter that she was clothed in scarlet? Now how is scarlet going to keep her and the family warm? So of course, the researcher in me was so intrigued by this that I had to dig deeper. I found out that scarlet is not only provocatively beautiful, but it is also associated with courage, force, passion, heat and joy. Need I say more?

Proverbs 31:22 *she makes covings for her bed she is clothed in fine linen and purple.*

Her home is put together with beautiful decorations. The bedroom is an impeccable utopia. Everything is put in its place. She looks good and fashionable wearing her purple royal garments around the house made from her fine linen line.

Proverbs 31:23 *Her Husband is respected at the city gate where he takes his seat among the elders of the land.*

Note: Her mate is respected which means he matches her. This means she has a man of good character, reputation, and he's about his business. He is a purpose walker like her. He creates, receives Heavenly downloads, walks by faith, command his day, surrounds himself with wisdom, and allows the Elders to mentor him… just like her. That means

28

he's not a career criminal out here doing dirty deals. He's not a womanizer out here chasing skirts. He's a man of respect and valor, attending to his father's business and madly in love with his wife. 360 woman, chose your man, your equal wisely.

Proverbs 31:24 *she makes fine linen garments and sells them, and supplies the merchants with sashes.*

She's back to business, using her gifted hands to make linen garments to sell them to the merchants. Wow! This 360 woman is an employer, buyer, inventor, developer, custom designer, wholesaler, importer, exporter, and chain supplier to the high-end store chains around the world. She always thinks about the bigger picture!

Note: Go big or go home!

Notes

What comes up for you after reading this chapter? Take a moment to reflect on what you read and record your thoughts.

_____

_____

_____

_____

_____

_____

_____

_____

_____

_____

_____

_____

_____

_____

_____

_____

_____

_____

_____

_____

_____

_____

Chapter Four

Proverbs 31:25 *she is clothed with strength and dignity; she can laugh at the days to come.*

She is drenched in righteousness. She's obedient and God is attached to her obedience. She is proud to obey and follow God's instructions and because of this he has crowned her with strength and dignity. And because of her lifestyle of obedience all these things have been added unto her.

(Matthew 6:33) *but seek Ye first the kingdom of God and all his righteousness; and all these things shall be added unto you.*

(Psalms 28:7) *The Joy of the Lord is her strength this is why she can laugh at the days to come because she knows it's all good.*

Proverbs 31:26 *She speaks with wisdom and faithful instruction is on her tongue.*

I find that wise people cannot sit and have idle conversation. They are drawn to conversations that bear fruit/seed, uplift, and produce change. What comes out of their mouths is always wise life-altering information. This 360 woman has faithful information. She mentors and consults those that hunger for it. She's always ready for the opportunity to plant seeds of wisdom. She doesn't over talk. She understands the cut on and the cut off.

Proverbs 31:27 *She watches over the affairs of her household and does not eat the bread of idleness.*

She is the household overseer. She's always in her household loop. She knows what's going on with her husband, her children, and her staff. She keeps the foundation of her household steady. She also refuses to do gossip so no Wendy Williams for her! She guards her gates… eyes, ears, nose, and mouth.

Proverbs 31:28 *Her children arise and call her blessed; her husband also and he praises her:*

There is no greater feeling in the world to a hard-working mother than the respect of her kids and the praise of her family. It is what sunlight is to a flower because of her sacrifice, her way of life, being a living example in home and outside of the home. I adore the part of her man praising her, being proud of his awesome wife with his chest poked out. He can't wait to get her alone so he can ravish her body and make love to her, speaking praises in her ears, giving her life. He says to his beautiful wife in Proverbs 31:29 Many women do noble things, but you surpass them all.

I imagine her husband being not just a lover but a cerebral lover, ravishing her mind, telling her how proud of his Queen he is, how beautiful she is, and just pouring continuous seed into her ears. He lets her know that her obedience to God turns him on.

Proverbs 31:30 *Charms is deceptive, and beauty is fleeting; but a woman that fears the Lord is to be praised.*

Her husband is captivated with her mission and honors her. He sees past her beauty and fine garments, but he sees her heart, her spirit, how precious and selfless she is, and he falls in love with her over and over again. She praises her King back and calls him Sire. It intoxicates him. He is drunken off of her language of love which is expressed through her actions that touches the depths of his heart.

Notes

What comes up for you after reading this chapter? Take a moment to reflect on what you read and record your thoughts.

_____

_____

_____

_____

_____

_____

_____

_____

_____

_____

_____

_____

_____

_____

_____

_____

_____

_____

_____

_____

Finale

Proverbs 31:31 *Honor her for all that her hands have done, and let her works bring her praise in the city gates.*

There is so much more that I'd like to expound on with this Proverbs 31 woman, but I will save that for volume 2. I want to leave you with these nuggets/insights.

What you put into the spirit, you should be able to pull out into the natural, on to the pavement, and create full manifestation because what goes up, must come down.

This noble 360 woman didn't choose this path for the money, she did this because she wanted to be obedient to God. She remembered Joshua 1:7-9, your obedience creates success in your life.

This 360 Queen Goddess is a Downloader.

She stays in download mode.

She's addicted to the downloading. Why? Because it's the download, the consistent staying in the spirit realm that placed her in the great position that she is in and got her the husband and the amazing life of peace, happiness, and wealth that she has.

She gives all honor to God for all things.

Insight allows her to see into the future to invent, takeover, and be consistent.

If she doesn't download, she doesn't know what to give the people she knows and understands she has to stay in the Spirit to be successful.

Notes

What comes up for you after reading this chapter? Take a moment to reflect on what you read and record your thoughts.

_____

_____

_____

_____

_____

_____

_____

_____

_____

_____

_____

_____

_____

_____

_____

_____

_____

_____

_____

_____

_____

360 Training Exercise Training

She's a Lover

A Focuser… A finisher

She's a dynamo: an extremely energetic person, a generator.

Wherever she goes she generates wealth /prosperity.

What does a 360 woman do in a dilemma? She prays! She prays the Word over her life until she manifests the resolution she needs. She never stops pressing. Even through her pain, she still pushes forward saying out loud, it must come to pass, it will come to pass.

How does she deal with her loneliness? She begins to walk in pursuit of purpose. When she's walking out purpose, she fills her spirit man up so there is no room or thought of loneliness.

She finds that her true companion is her purpose, and she lives to fulfill it.

"Stay Blessed, Stay Focused, Know your purpose"

(Raja)

Are You a 360 Woman?

Use the following pages to do a self-assessment. In each section, reflect on where you are and what changes you need to make to become or grow as a 360 Woman.

Proverbs 10:1-2 *"A wife a woman of noble character, who can find her?"*

_____

_____

_____

_____

"She selects wool and flax and works eagerly with her hands. She is like merchant ships, bringing her food from afar." **-Proverbs 31:13-14 NIV**

_____

_____

_____

_____

Proverbs 31:15 *"She gets up while it is still night,..."*

_____

_____

_____

_____

"She considers a field and buys it; out of her own earnings she plants a vineyard." **-Proverbs 31:16 NIV**

_____

_____

_____

_____

Proverbs 31:17 *"She sets about her work vigorously, her arms are strong for her task."*

_____

_____

_____

_____

Proverbs 31:18, *"She is so pleased with her business dealings she knows she did well, and her lamp does not go out at night."*

_____

_____

_____

_____

Proverbs 31:19 *"...in her hands she holds the distaff, and grasped the spindle with her fingers..."*

_____

_____

_____

_____

Proverbs 31:20 *"...she opens her arms to the poor and extends her hands to the needy...."*

_____

_____

_____

_____

Proverbs 31:21 *When it snows, she has no fear for her household; for all of them are clothed in scarlet.*

_____

_____

_____

_____

Proverbs 31:22 *"she makes covings for her bed she is clothed in fine linen and purple."*

_____

_____

_____

_____

Proverbs 31:23 *"Her Husband is respected at the city gate where he takes his seat among the elders of the land."*

_____

_____

_____

_____

Proverbs 31:24 *"she makes fine linen garments and sells them, and supplies the merchants with sashes."*

_____

_____

_____

_____

Proverbs 31:25 *"she is clothed with strength and dignity; she can laugh at the days to come."*

_____

_____

_____

_____

Proverbs 31:26 *"She speaks with wisdom and faithful instruction is on her tongue."*

_____

_____

_____

_____

Proverbs 31:27 *"She watches over the affairs of her household and does not eat the bread of idleness."*

_____

_____

_____

_____

Proverbs 31:28 *"Her children arise and call her blessed; her husband also and he praises her:"*

_____

_____

_____

_____

Proverbs 31:30 *"Charms is deceptive, and beauty is fleeting; but a woman that fears the Lord is to be praised."*

_____

_____

_____

_____